BRITAIN IN OLD PHOTOGRAPHS

TOTT████M, HORNSEY & WOOD GREEN

D0863927

CHRIS PROTZ

SUTTON PUBLISHING LIMITED

❄ **HARINGEY** COUNCIL ❄

Sutton Publishing Limited
Phoenix Mill · Thrupp · Stroud
Gloucestershire · GL5 2BU

First published 1998

Cover photographs. Front: opening day of the
electric tram service, Wood Green to Finsbury
Park, 1904. Back: children learning road safety
at the model traffic area, Lordship Lane Park,
Tottenham, *c*. 1950.
Title page photograph: The Pound, Highgate,
opposite Broadlands Road, *c*. 1880.

British Library Cataloguing in Publication Data
A catalogue record for this book is available from the
British Library.

ISBN 0-7509-1295-2

Typeset in 10/12 Perpetua.
Typesetting and origination by
Sutton Publishing Limited.
Printed in Great Britain by
Ebenezer Baylis, Worcester.

ACKNOWLEDGEMENTS

This book would not have been possible without the support and help of the staff at Bruce
Castle. My thanks in particular to Penny Wheatcroft, the curator, who supported and advised on
this project, and to the local history officer, Rita Read, who provided so much of the
information I needed. I am also grateful for their generosity in allowing me access to the wealth
of photographs in the Haringey archives at Bruce Castle. My regret is that I could use only a
fraction of the pictures for this book. I would particularly like to record my thanks to Peter
Curtis, who started the work on these photographs. Although he died before he could develop
the work further, I hope he would have appreciated the eventual outcome.

Devonshire Hill Lane, Tottenham, 1907

CONTENTS

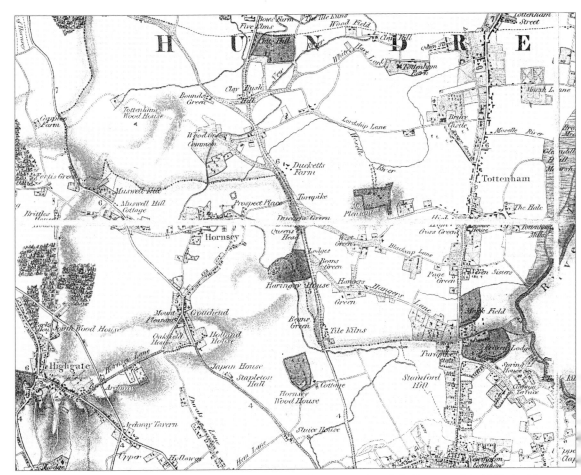

Extract from Greenwood's map of Middlesex, published by G. Pringle and C. Greenwood in 1819. At this date, Tottenham was still part of the administrative district of Edmonton Hundred while Highgate and Hornsey were in the Hundred of Ossulstone. The villages and hamlets which eventually formed Tottenham, Hornsey and Wood Green are already established, as are many of the main roads. We see here a rural area of farms and woods, and the estates of large houses. However, the growth of London is already noticeable in Tottenham's ribbon development along the High Road north of Stamford Hill, while over to the west, Highgate village mirrors a similar growth along the Great North Road.

INTRODUCTION

In 1965 the metropolitan boroughs of Tottenham, Hornsey and Wood Green amalgamated to form the London Borough of Haringey and the district became part of the metropolis. The city's urban sprawl had accelerated in the nineteenth and twentieth centuries to engulf the rural communities on its outskirts. In that time the pretty hamlets and villages of Middlesex experienced a dizzying transformation from countryside to town, from suburbia to city. This book records some of that transformation.

There were settlements in Haringey at least from Anglo-Saxon times, particularly in the east where the banks of the River Lea allowed easy cultivation and the river itself convenient transportation. Tottenham developed early along the old Roman road of Ermine Street, running north from London, and is mentioned in the Domesday Book. Small settlements grew up around High Cross and the Hale and the open greens now remembered only by their names, such as Scotland Green and Page Green. By 1850 Tottenham was a large village, spreading along the High Road and westwards up Philip Lane and West Green Road. As well as the farms and industries of a rural community, there were large houses, such as Bruce Castle in Lordship Lane, Tottenham Park along White Hart Lane and Mountpleasant House near Philip Lane. These were homes to wealthy Londoners looking for a country retreat, as were the more modest houses lining the High Road. Daniel Defoe commented on this early ribbon development, noting that the road from London to Enfield 'seems to the traveller to be one continuous street, especially Tottenham and Edmonton'. The High Road was also a coaching road and as such had a substantial number of inns, many of which, such as the Plough and the Swan, survive in name if not in building.

To the west the Borough is bounded by the Northern Heights and here the thick oak forest that once covered all of present-day Haringey was slow to disappear. The manors of Hornsey were held by the Bishops of London and much of the area was retained as woodland and used for hunting. The parish developed slowly in small distinct settlements. The main Hornsey village was along the High Street and around St Mary's parish church, with hamlets at Crouch End, Muswell Hill and Stroud Green. Even by the 1860s these districts showed little evidence of urban development, while Muswell Hill remained a remote farming community until the 1890s. Highgate village, only part of which is in Hornsey, developed differently, however. Its location on the Great North Road out of London, as well as the healthier environment of the Northern Heights, gave rise to the development of the village as a residential area for wealthy Londoners. It consequently showed a pattern of early housebuilding similar to that in Tottenham.

In Wood Green the forest, known as Tottenham Wood, was gradually cleared for farmland by the end of the eighteenth century, but there was little housing development until the second half of the nineteenth. The hamlet was a remote part of Tottenham parish joined to the main village by Lordship Lane, an unbuilt country lane till the end of the century. In 1844 the Chapel of St Michaels, Bounds Green, was built, and in 1863 Tottenham Wood farmlands were converted into the leisure grounds of Alexandra Park. These developments, together with the opening of Wood Green station in 1859 on the Great Northern railway line out of King's Cross, contributed to the growth of Wood Green. By the 1870s a substantial community had grown up in the triangle of land formed by Bounds Green Road and Green Lanes. In 1888 it had grown sufficiently to achieve formal separation from Tottenham as a local government district.

The various communities of present-day Haringey experienced urbanisation differently according to both geography and the lines of communication. Tottenham, with its location on the main road from London to Hertfordshire, had already grown substantially by the nineteenth century. By the middle of that century it had become an attractive residential area for middle-class Londoners, although it was still largely rural until the 1880s. A dramatic change followed the opening in 1872 of the Great Eastern railway line from Liverpool Street to Enfield, with stations at Bruce Grove, Seven Sisters and White Hart Lane. The line offered cheap workmen's tickets, and stimulated the movement of people from the overcrowded streets of Hackney and the East End to the suburbs of Tottenham. An intensive period of housebuilding followed, breaking up the old estates and replacing them with speculative building. The flat, low-lying land of Tottenham supported the development of narrow streets of terraced housing, and by the turn of the century it had become a predominantly lower middle- and working-class area. Industry soon followed, also driven out of London by high rents and lack of space. The open fields of the Lea valley were attractive to industrial development, and this area sustained a level of industrialisation not experienced further west.

The opening of the Great Northern railway line from King's Cross, running along the eastern edge of Hornsey and through Wood Green, affected growth in the west more slowly. A further impetus came about with the later opening of branch lines. The Palace Gates line from Wood Green to Finsbury Park was opened in 1878, also stimulating development in the small hamlet of West Green. In 1867 Crouch End and Highgate were linked to Finsbury Park on the branch line to Edgware and a further station was added at Stroud Green in 1881. The final three decades of the nineteenth century witnessed the rapid growth of Hornsey, Crouch End, Stroud Green and Wood Green as the estates of large houses, such as Crouch Hall, Topsfield Hall and Harringay House, gave way to commuter suburbs. The development of these western districts differed substantially in character from Tottenham. A combination of high ground and vigorous campaigning from the local community, as well as the lack of cheap fares on the railways, led to the growth of villa residences and superior terraced housing in wide streets. This, together with the absence of any significant industry, gave rise to Hornsey and Wood Green as middle-class commuter suburbs, apart from the specific development of the Noel Park Estate on the flatter area east of Green Lanes.

In spite of this rapid growth during the latter half of the nineteenth century, not all the district was laid down for streets and housing. In Tottenham, the area between Lordship Lane and the Edmonton border, including White Hart Lane, remained rural. Land on the western side of the railway in Wood Green was open, including Alexandra Park, while Muswell Hill still awaited its Edwardian development. This development, together with that of the remaining open spaces, could not be resisted. By the 1930s Haringey was largely built up. All that now remains of its forests, farmlands and large estates are the woods of Highgate, Queens and Coldfall in the west, and the parks and sports grounds saved for leisure use by local authority intervention.

CHAPTER ONE

FORGOTTEN SCENES

The open fields and farmlands of Haringey's villages, such as these of Mount Pleasant Fields, Tottenham, have long since given way to streets and houses. This picture was taken in 1892, when the cutting for Mount Pleasant Road, running across the field, signalled the housing development to come. In front are three gypsy children, with their caravan in the background. Their families could still get some casual farm work in the locality, as this chapter will show, but were more likely to seek their opportunities from the developing trades, commerce and entertainment recorded in the later chapters.

An engraving showing a rural Hornsey village in 1750. Cows remained a feature of the area well into urban times, providing fresh milk for local residents.

Tottenham village in 1822, as painted by George Scharf, appears less pastoral, as the village was on the main road from London to the north. The old Swan public house, recorded with delight by Isaak Walton in his *Compleat Angler*, is on the left, and the High Cross monument on the right (see p. 144).

This early view of Tottenham Lane in Hornsey was taken around 1860 by George Shadbolt, a local amateur photographer and one of the pioneers of early photography. Many of his pictures, taken between 1850 and 1865, were of Hornsey village, Crouch End and Muswell Hill. This picture, a salted paper print, shows Tottenham Lane looking south. The building to the right was St Mary's Infants' School, now the headquarters of Hornsey Historical Society. The cottages to the left – Manor Cottages – were not demolished until 1928.

This picture by Shadbolt of Hornsey village in the mid-nineteenth century shows clapboard houses, barns and a shop. It is taken looking north, with the High Street running through the centre of the village. The road travels over the New River to the left, where a wooden bridge can be seen. The New River, dug in 1613 to bring water to London, crosses under Hornsey High Street in three places. It has, however, long been straightened and culverted over to remain largely hidden from sight.

Mount Pleasant Pond in this albumen print by Shadbolt is largely obscured by shrubs and trees. The pond, at the foot of Mount Pleasant, and east of Crouch Hill, is now the site of the junction between Mount Pleasant Villas and Blythwood Road.

Shadbolt's picture of Priory Road shows a footbridge crossing one of the many local streams. This location is the present site of the junction of Priory Road and Middle Lane.

Rectory Farm, White Hart Lane, was the most scenic of local farms and was painted by the local artist, John Bonny (see p. 92). The farm, shown here in 1908, was opposite Tottenham Park, now the area around Weir Hall Road.

Spencer's Farm, formerly Turners Farm, in Hornsey Lane, stood at the top of Stanhope Lane. In 1883, when this picture was taken, it was already being hemmed in by housing development and later contracted to one field further up Stanhope Lane.

Broadwaters Farm, Lordship Lane, 1892. This was a dairy farm, as we see from the milk float and churns, and at this time it was occupied by Mr Andrews. The farm was sold to Tottenham Council in 1926 and converted to the Lido open air swimming pool.

Uptons Farm in Muswell Hill Road was also feeling the effect of housing development when this picture was taken around 1883. The farm, on the east side of the road, stretched from St James's Church to Queens Wood. It was sold as housing lots in 1894.

A salted paper print of hay carts taken by George Shadbolt around 1860. Until well into the nineteenth century, Hornsey consisted of pasture and meadow and the area was an important producer of hay for the London market.

A well-posed picture of workers haymaking in Highgate around 1880. The women are wearing straw hats to protect them from the sun and the men, also typically, wear hats or caps.

Dodd's Forge, on the corner of Highgate High Street and South Grove, 1895. The building was in a ramshackle state when sold by its last owner, John Dodd, and was demolished. There was a forge on this site from 1664 to 1895.

An 1890 postcard of Battersby's Forge. Standing at the junction of Crouch Hill and Crouch End Hill, it was demolished in 1895 following the sale of the Topsfield estate. It was replaced by the Westminster bank, opposite the King's Head public house.

Bruce Castle Park at the turn of the century, with a view across the now-vanished pond to All Hallows Church. The park was purchased by Tottenham Urban District Council in 1891 for public use.

The open waters of the Moselle Brook running through Scotland Green, pictured before it was culverted over in 1906. This view is looking east along Scotland Green, from the High Road. A horse and carriage crosses the bridge towards Hartington Road.

The weatherboarded walls and steeply pitched roof of the Laundress's Cottage, Hornsey, were typical of older buildings in the area. Many homes and commercial premises were wood-built before brick became dominant. This is another photograph taken by George Shadbolt.

Weatherboarded cottages behind the Rose and Crown in High Cross Road, 1893. The house to the left is being used as a bootmakers' shop by Oriel Vivash, one of the Jewish immigrants then in the area.

These weatherboarded shops in Tottenham High Road are shown shortly before they were demolished in 1907. The shops, opposite Bruce Grove station, were on the site now occupied by McDonald's, and before that Marks & Spencer (see p. 25).

Elijah King's shoe repair shop in Hornsey High Street, shortly before demolition in 1904. Called Jessamine Cottage, it was the last of several wooden cottages opposite the Green (now Hillfield Avenue) in Hornsey High Street.

The Royal Oak, St James's Lane, 1880. In the background are the arches of the Great Northern branch line from Highgate to Alexandra Palace. This line has since been closed and the land converted to the Parkland Walk.

A crowd of patrons outside the Ferry Boat Inn, Ferry Lane, 1891. The inn stood by the River Lea and was a popular place for local people enjoying outings and bank holidays. The sign above the door reads 'Ye Old Ferrie Boat, Subscription Fishery'.

The original Hope and Anchor, Tottenham Lane, in 1888, before it was rebuilt in the 1890s. Two proud owners of penny-farthing bicycles stand at the front with a policeman.

The Plough Tavern, Tottenham High Road, was originally built in 1537. It is shown here in 1886 before rebuilding in 1892. The yearly meetings of the Tottenham Court Leet were held at the Plough until 1886. Brook Street Chapel is on the left.

The Green Man in Muswell Hill was extended soon after this picture was taken in 1880. The name of this old public house probably reflects a time when the area was used for hunting. It is likely there has been an inn on this site for many centuries.

Park Road, Hornsey, c. 1900. The picture is taken from the corner of Wolsey Road looking towards Crouch End and includes the China Cup Working Men's Club and a coffee house.

A group of shoppers and residents pose for a photograph along Crouch End Hill in 1890. This view is looking up to Hornsey Lane from The Broadway at the junction of Crouch Hill. The King's Head, demolished and rebuilt in 1892, is to the right. The spire of Christchurch, built in 1863, can be seen in the distance. Crouch End developed as a thriving suburb in the last two decades of the nineteenth century following the opening of Crouch End station in 1867.

(Opposite, top) Ives Coffee House and Dumbletons Hatters, pictured here in 1892, occupy the former premises of the Old Blue Lion Tavern in Tottenham High Road. The tavern was built in 1500 and the building destroyed by fire in 1894. The plate indicating the parish boundary with Edmonton is on the left of the building.

(Opposite, bottom) By 1901 Wood Green High Road had become a main shopping thoroughfare. This view, looking north, with Mayes Road on the left, is now the site of Wood Green shopping city.

Bruce Grove, Tottenham, 1893. It was a handsome, tree-lined street, with Georgian houses on the west side and fields opposite. This picture shows nos 11 to 14, which are still standing. A milk delivery cart is in the road.

This picture by A. Close of Tottenham shows the elms along Bruce Grove being felled in 1903 to make way for more buildings. The railway bridge by Bruce Grove station can be seen in the distance to the right.

CHAPTER TWO

DEVELOPING THE URBAN COMMUNITY

*As compensation for the loss of the trees and fields, the local community
gained a number of opportunities and improved facilities. Better paid
and more regular work was available, attracting greater numbers of
people to the area and giving rise to the consumer society. Shopping,
such as at Marks & Spencer's Bazaar, became more varied and attractive.
This shop, built in 1907 on the terrace that replaced the weatherboarded
shops shown on p. 18, soon expanded to larger premises alongside. With
the growth of the consumer society, local shopping areas, such as
Tottenham and Wood Green High Roads, flourished, with chain stores,
department stores and grocery chains. Their contraction, following out-
of-town developments, is another story.*

The modern answer to the problems of urban waste was this refuse destructor, built in 1908 on the site of the old Moat House by Wood Green Common. Here we see a solitary workman shovelling the waste on the feeding floor.

Workmen and their overseer pose for a picture during the culverting of the Moselle Brook in 1906. They are probably working on the section known as Carbuncle Alley near Scotland Green. The Moselle was gradually culverted over in sections from 1836, but can be seen briefly in Lordship Recreation Ground and Tottenham Cemetery. Streams rising further west caused considerable problems of flooding in Tottenham and Wood Green. As Fisk recorded in his *History of Tottenham* (1913): 'Any exceptional downpour of rain in Muswell Hill always caused trouble to Tottenham.'

This early picture by George Shadbolt shows brickmaking in Hornsey in the mid-nineteenth century. The horse-driven pug mill on the right is used to blend the clay.

This picture of a brickfield near Archway Road in 1880 illustrates the quantity of bricks being produced and the heavy demand for labour. Brickmaking was once a common industry in the locality, exploiting the London clay to build the houses and shops of the growing suburbs.

A workman displays the different sizes of pot produced by South's Pottery, *c.* 1927. As well as bricks, the local clay was also used to produce pots for the market gardening industry around London. Samuel South & Sons was a long-established family firm in White Hart Lane.

W.T. Williamson & Sons pottery works, Green Lanes, Harringay, 1897. This view, taken after a flood, is looking south-east and shows stacks of glazed pipes near the main road, with a cottage beyond.

Williamson's Cottages were condemned as 'unfit for human habitation' by the Medical Officer of Health in 1905. These cottages, probably those in the picture on p. 29, were affected by the overflow of the nearby stream. They stood on the west side of Green Lanes, near the Beaconsfield public house.

Old cottages in Albert Place, Tottenham High Road, before they were repaired in 1893. They stood next to the site presently occupied by Peacock's, and before that Woolworth's.

This decaying terrace of cottages in Markfield Road, south Tottenham, were little more than fifty years old when this picture was taken around 1912. Neglect had left the bay windows badly cracked, and the shop at the end is barely standing.

Wooden cottages in Scotland Green, pictured in 1933, shortly before slum clearance. These cottages were part of the densely inhabited alleyways of this old district, including Tubby's Alley, Ward's Alley and Stack Yard.

Burgess Yard, Waggon Lane, pictured shortly before slum clearance in 1932. Waggon Lane was a narrow old road – just 11 ft wide – stretching from Tottenham High Road to Willoughby Lane. The High Road end was densely packed with twenty-seven houses, including Burgess Yard, which were probably built in the first half of the nineteenth century. A narrow alleyway leading to Waggon Lane is on the right of the children.

Better quality workers' houses are shown here in Farrant Avenue on the Noel Park Estate, Wood Green. They were built from 1883 onwards by the Artizans, Labourers & General Dwellings Company for London workers moving out to the better area of Wood Green.

Like the Noel Park homes, these artisan houses in Reform Row, Tottenham, are still standing. The houses, shown here in 1907, faced an open green, and posts for tethering horses can be seen in the road.

Some of the houses in Reform Row were owned by the builders merchant, G.L. Wilson & Co., founded in 1877. The growth of Tottenham and villages to the north along the River Lea depended on an efficient supply of materials, such as was provided by this family firm in Tottenham High Road. This steam van, pictured in 1914, records the firm's various depots. Wilson's experimented early with alternatives to horse-drawn transport, choosing steam first as motor lorries were then unreliable.

J.A. Prestwich's engineering factory was founded in 1895 in Northumberland Park. First manufacturing scientific instruments, by the turn of the century they were producing motor cycles, cars – and even aeroplanes. A monoplane built by JAP in 1909 is in the Science Museum, Kensington.

JAP moved from scientific instruments to motor bikes in 1903, starting with 2.5 hp air-cooled models. This publicity picture of their racing bikes records '200 Firsts and 50 World Records'.

Interior of J.A. Prestwich's factory, *c.* 1910. The young apprentices are working on complex machinery. They are all wearing collars and ties beneath their overalls, in the fashion of the time.

Women working in Crusha's the Printers, Tottenham High Road, *c*. 1900. Crusha's printed the long-established *Tottenham and Edmonton Weekly Herald*. Founded in 1861, the *Herald* was acquired by Edwin Crusha in 1864. This family firm also published the *Wood Green and Southgate Weekly Herald*. Crusha family members were very active in the local community.

Flatau's shoe factory in Tottenham Hale, 1905. This factory, on the corner of Broad Lane and Ferry Lane, was established by the brothers Abraham and William Flatau in 1900. The Hope and Anchor public house is to the left.

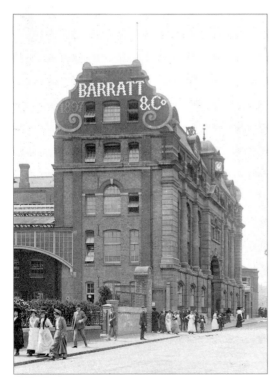

Barratt's sweet factory in Western Road was an important employer of women, and one of the few large-scale factories in Wood Green. It opened in 1880, having moved from Islington, and closed in the 1980s.

William Edward Gardner with his milk float and boy in West Beech Road, Wood Green, *c.* 1905. In the days before refrigeration milk in open churns was taken round the streets up to three times a day.

Carcasses on display outside a butcher's shop at High Cross, 1870. Before refrigeration, housewives would often shop just before closing time to buy meat sold at a reduced price before it went bad.

Drawmer's tea warehouse, 456 High Road, Tottenham, 1910. The shop advertises its own local tea, the Bruce Castle blend. Albert Place (see p. 30) can be seen to the right. The site is now occupied by Peacock's store.

Mammen's shoe shop in Seven Sisters Road, *c*. 1910. Mr Harry Mammen (centre) was active in the local community as secretary, and later treasurer, of the Enterprise Club, Page Green.

St Michael's Terrace in Wood Green was a thriving commercial centre in 1902. The terrace was close to Wood Green railway station, and the local shops included dining rooms, printers and stationers, an estate agent's and a cycle shop.

Commerce Road, Wood Green, was another busy area at this time. The earliest part of Wood Green to develop in the 1860s was the triangle of land between Bounds Green Road and Green Lanes, including Commerce, Nightingale and Truro Roads.

This picture was taken at the junction of Philip Lane and Tottenham High Road one early morning in 1905. To the left is the row of shops between The Swan and the public library (partially hidden). The Rose and Crown, with three magnificent gas lamps, is to the right.

This picture was taken in 1935 to commemorate the introduction of electric lights along Wood Green High Road. Electric lighting replaced the gas lamps seen above.

CHAPTER THREE

RIVER, ROAD & RAIL

Transport both promoted and followed the growth of Haringey. Railways in particular stimulated development, facilitating travel to work as well as the more efficient distribution of industrial and commercial products. But although railways had a more dramatic impact on growth than the older types of river and road transport, their lack of flexibility had to give way to the innovations of the motor engine. Road transport, with its greater diversity and access to an ever-expanding network of local and national roads, became the dominant form of transport. Here we see the last steam train leaving Alexandra Park station in July 1954 after the closure of the Northern Heights branch line to Highgate.

Snow scene at Tottenham Lock, River Lea, 1893. The River Lea canal, running from Hertfordshire to the Thames, was an important method of transporting heavy goods, such as wood and coal, by barge.

An engine-driven boat clearing the ice on the River Lea near Tottenham Hale in 1893. The horses on the left have a break from pulling the barges until the way is clear.

Barge horses resting by the lockkeeper's house at Tottenham Lock in 1958. The tall chimney of the Eagle pencil factory appears in the distance.

The number of barges waiting to go through Tottenham lock shows that this was still a much-used form of transport for heavy goods as recently as the 1950s. The picture shows the Ferry Lane bridge, with a trolley bus crossing.

Laying tarblocks in Tottenham High Road, 1904. The main roads were covered with blocks of tar laid by hand; discarded blocks were popular with local residents as fuel for their fires. The Quaker meeting hall is in the background, with the old Sanchez Almshouses on the right (see p. 140).

Horse-drawn wagons on Tottenham High Road, 1900. Horses continued to be the main method of transporting goods well into the twentieth century. The brewery dray on the left is delivering barrels to one of many public houses along the High Road.

Laying the tramlines on Highgate Hill, *c.* 1884. These lines were being laid in preparation for the cable cars to help tackle the challenging gradient of Highgate Hill.

A horse-drawn tram in Tottenham High Road, *c.* 1895. This double-decker, pulled by three horses, replaced the single-decker trams of the 1880s. There had been considerable opposition from influential local inhabitants to laying the tramlines, but trams substantially improved urban mobility.

A steam tram waiting at Seven Sisters, *c.* 1890. This first attempt to use more modern technology to supplant horses was not entirely successful; the trams broke down frequently, and proved both smelly and dirty. Steam trams ran in Tottenham from 1885 to 1891, but the engine (a Merryweather) was then taken to Birmingham, where apparently it was quite successful. The steam company went into liquidation in 1891 and the tram lines returned to horse-drawn traffic, with the double-decker shown in the previous picture.

(Opposite top) The opening day of the Finsbury Park to Wood Green tram service in 1904. Tram no. 109 is a Metropolitan Electric Tramways Company Type A vehicle with the power supplied through overhead lines.

(Opposite bottom) This postcard shows an even more streamlined electric tram at Spouters Corner in High Road, Wood Green, *c.* 1910. The upper deck is still open to the elements: until 1926 the police objected to covered tops on the grounds of safety.

The no. 29 bus route was started by the Admiral Garage, Willow Walk, Turnpike Lane. The driver, shown here in 1914, is Robert Russell. Buses, not being confined to tramlines, were able to develop different routes, leading to a greater expansion of public transport.

A London General Omnibus Company (LGDC) bus in Stroud Green Road, 1914. Running from Finsbury Park to Muswell Hill, this single-decker bus was designed for the North London route which crossed bridges not built to carry heavy traffic.

'Ole Bill' bus in Wood Green Garage. This old bus, similar to that shown opposite, is being used for the funeral of a Transport Board employee in 1961. By this time the various private routes had been brought together under the publicly owned London Transport Board. The bus lists significant First World War battles, where many former transport workers had fought and perhaps died.

A 'Feltham tram' (right) and a bus going to Victoria station negotiate the floods in Green Lanes in 1937. The spire of Harringay Congregational church on the corner of Allison Road can be seen in the background.

Between the 1930s and the 1960s trolley buses replaced trams, but still used their overhead wires. The driver of this bus, seen in Broad Lane, is a learner on the Manor House to Ilford route, opened in 1936.

A 'growler' cab waiting for passengers outside Crouch End station in 1900. Opened in 1867, the station was on the Edgware, Highgate and London line from the City and opened the way for the development of the district as a commuter suburb.

Bruce Grove station, on the Liverpool Street to Enfield line, pictured in 1911. The opening of this line in 1872, with cheap workmen's tickets, was a key factor in the growth of Tottenham as an urban area.

The last passenger train leaves Palace Gates station in 1963. This line, opened in 1878, went to Seven Sisters junction. Palace Gates, between Wood Green station and Bounds Green Road, was close to Barratt's factory. The railway stimulated Wood Green's growth and separation from Tottenham.

A guard signals the last passenger train at Cranley Gardens station in 1954. This station, on the branch line from Highgate to Alexandra Palace, was opened in 1902.

These shops and offices were pulled down in 1930 to make way for Wood Green underground station. The development of the station has radically altered the appearance of this junction between Wood Green High Road and Lordship Lane.

Workmen sink the preliminary shaft for the underground at Wood Green in 1930. The extension of the Piccadilly line from Finsbury Park through Wood Green to Cockfosters was an important development in the economy and transport of the area. It stimulated the growth of Wood Green as a commercial centre.

Wood Green station, 1932. Typical 1930s architecture replaces the Victorian shops of the earlier picture. We also get our first glimpse of a car waiting outside the station.

Turnpike Lane station, 1948. This was a more spacious development than Wood Green, with a bus terminus and shops alongside. A J. Lyons' café was also included, with its reputation for good inexpensive teas and light meals.

CHAPTER FOUR

LIFE & LEISURE

The Ferry Boat Inn by the banks of the River Lea was a popular place for outings, especially on a bank holiday such as this one in 1886. A brass band played in the nearby gardens (Day's Dancing Grounds) and there were fairs over the adjoining marshes as well as fishing in the Lea. Working people had fewer holidays in these earlier decades, but they still took every opportunity to enjoy themselves. There were older pursuits such as dancing or cricket, or the more modern cinema and cycling. Even at work there were also opportunities for socialising and enjoyment, as we shall see on the following pages.

Cricketers on Tottenham Marshes, *c.* 1865. They are wearing a variety of sports gear – and hats! – and are probably a team of local tradesmen. The marshes were popular for organised sports, including football and tennis, as well as cricket, until the Second World War.

Skaters on the marshes in the winter of 1928/9. Young men and boys take the opportunity to skate on the frozen floodwater from the River Lea. The Lea flooded regularly before the banks were built up.

'The team that visited Holland', Tottenham Cricket Club in 1890. It was a very successful tour. They played four matches and were 'easy winners of three'. The top scorer was F. Perrin, pictured holding the bat in the front row. Back row, left to right: E. Thomas, W.W. Mortlock, J.G. Webb, C. Lovebond, E.H. Watson, J.F. Mayo. Second row: A.A. Robinson, W.G. Mortlock, H.T. Burton (captain). Front row: A. Endean, G. Bell, F. Perrin, C. Toy, A. Rodda.

Hornsey playing fields in Park Road were leased to sports clubs by the Ecclesiastical Commissioners from 1892. This picture, taken at the turn of the century, shows the substantial number of men, boys and horses needed to keep the playing fields in peak condition.

Tottenham Cycling Club, 1898. This picture reflects the popularity of cycling at the time following the introduction of the chain-operated safety cycle and Dunlop's pneumatic tyre. Bicycles offered the opportunity for men, women and children to travel on outings to the countryside. The bikes were equipped with large horns: pedestrians, unused to these speedy and silent vehicles, could often be in danger.

Wood Green Cycle Track in 1895, demonstrating a more active use of cycles. This track, opened in 1895 by C.P. Sisley, held cycle races and international meetings. Its chief sponsor was A.W. Gamage, owner of the then famous City department store. However, the track closed in 1900, when a more profitable use of the land was found for building development. Built on the site of Nightingale Hall, the track was replaced by Cornwall, Braemar and Northcote Avenues.

Football crowds leaving the Spurs ground in Tottenham High Road, *c.* 1905. The club, which turned professional in 1895, first played on this ground in 1899. Before that they played on Tottenham Marshes. This picture was taken from the roof of Hunnings the printers at 516 High Road.

Tottenham Hotspur football club, 1919/20. The club was founded in 1882 as an amateur team by a group of cricketers who did not want to lose touch over the winter months.

The Palace Theatre of Varieties, Tottenham High Road, opened in 1908 as a music hall theatre with seats for up to 1,500 people. Reflecting popular culture, it became a picture house and then a bingo hall, before closing in the 1980s. The building now houses a church.

The Canadian Rink in Tottenham High Road, 1910. Situated next to the Palace, this also reflected changes in popular culture: starting as a skating rink, it then became a dance hall and is now a nightclub.

The Wood Green Empire, built in 1912 with seats for up to 1,850 people, had a London-wide reputation for music hall and variety acts. The Empire was built in the Edwardian section of shops along Wood Green High Road known as Cheapside. It closed as a theatre in 1955 and the building was redeveloped. It is now Sainsbury's supermarket, with its entrance in Lymington Avenue, and the frontage is a building society.

The Premier Electric Theatre in Frobisher Road, Wood Green, opened in 1910. It went through several changes of name (Regal and Essoldo), before briefly becoming a bingo hall (the Vogue) in 1963. It is now a cinema again, the Curzon, specialising in Hindi films.

Bruce Grove cinema, shown here in 1939, was opened in 1921 by local people, who formed a company, the Tottenham Cinema and Entertainment Co. It also included a dance hall. It has long since closed and the building is now occupied by a snooker hall and a church.

The Athenaeum in Fortis Green was built by
James Edmonson in 1900, along with the shops
of St James's Parade. It provided two halls for
literary, scientific and social activities for the
new suburb of Muswell Hill. The site is now
occupied by Sainsbury's supermarket.

Studio interior of Hornsey School of Art, Crouch End, *c.* 1900. Founded as a private school by Frank
Swinstead in 1882, it offered full-time places and some boarding, as well as part-time and evening classes.

The Shell Bandstand in Lordship Recreation Ground, 1950. The park was built on the site of Broadwater Farm (see p. 13) and the Shell was erected in 1936 by the local council to provide facilities for music, dance and drama. Here we see a small band playing, and several very elegant couples dancing in front.

This picture of a fair in Bruce Castle Park was taken by a member of Tottenham Camera Club before the Second World War. The Club has provided us with many informal pictures of pre-war Tottenham.

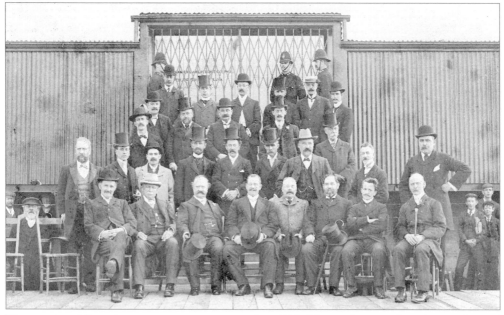

The opening of Tottenham open air swimming pool in 1905. This pool, situated on the marshes and drawing its water straight from the River Lea, was one of the first in the area. It was demolished in 1938, following the opening of Tottenham Lido on Lordship Lane.

Alexandra Park open air swimming pool, 1926. The pool, built in 1907, complemented the Western Road pool by offering open air facilities in the summer. It was located between the racecourse and the reservoirs in the park.

Durnsford Road swimming pool, 1934. Most open air swimming pools have succumbed to the inclemency of English weather, but in the 1920s and '30s they were very popular. This pool offered accommodation for 502 men and 490 women. There is now a garden centre on the site.

Office and factory workers in the staff canteen of Gestetner's, *c.* 1940. The staff canteens of larger factories offered the welcome facility of prepared, subsidised meals eaten in the company of fellow workers. Usually workers had to eat their packed lunches at their workbench in the factory. Gestetner's was a highly successful business manufacturing all forms of office duplicating equipment, and it found a ready market in the twentieth-century expansion of office work (see p. 95).

The clerks and bureaucrats of Wood Green District Council relaxing on a staff outing in 1904. Wood Green had formerly been part of Tottenham, but in 1888, following petitions from local residents, it became a separate Board of Health district. Then in 1894 it became an Urban District Council, fully independent from Tottenham. These gentlemen may be celebrating ten years as a local authority, responsible for health, planning, elementary education and various civic amenities such as the refuse destructor shown on p. 26.

A rather more exciting outing for the workers of JAP's Tottenham factory. Pictured in a charabanc (the motorised version of the horse-drawn brake) outside the Northumberland Arms, they are waiting to go to the Spurs vs Chelsea Cup Final in 1925.

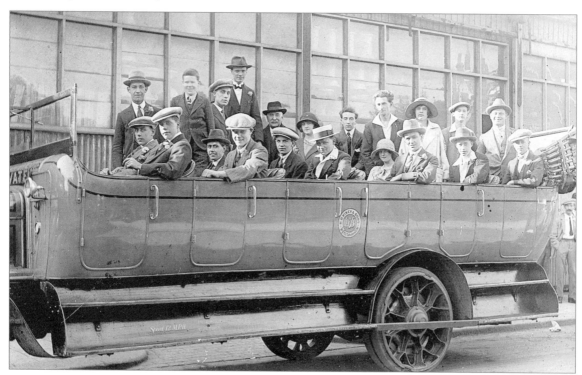

These workers from G.A. Wilson's were off to Clacton on Sea for their annual outing in 1924. These outings (known as 'Beanos') were a feature of factory life until they gradually died out at the end of the 1960s.

CHAPTER FIVE

SOME CHILDHOOD SCENES

A very orderly procession of schoolgirls passes Wilson's shop on Tottenham High Road at the turn of the century. This is typical of many of the pictures of childhood on the following pages, with disciplined school pictures, orderly park scenes and well-organised outings. But children being children, their rather less controlled side sometimes shines through!

This exhibition demonstrates the clothes worn by the pupils of the Blue School in Tottenham when it was a girls' charity school in the nineteenth century. White aprons and capes kept their clothes clean, while bonnets kept their hair neat and tidy.

The Blue School, Scotland Green, 1892. The school was established in 1735. This building was erected in 1833 and enlarged in 1876, when it was named the Middle Class School for Girls. It is still standing, with the ground floor now converted to shops.

The infants' class, Coleraine School, Tottenham, *c*. 1900. The children sit straight-backed, their arms folded neatly behind their backs. The girls wear white aprons and the boys display large collars. Note the educational charts and pictures on the walls.

Pupils at White Hart Lane Infants' School, *c*. 1900. They are demonstrating a drawing lesson – presumably a pair of cherries. The children wrote on slates with chalk, which could be rubbed off and the slates reused. The classroom rises steeply to the back.

Tiered desks in the classrooms in Crouch End School, Wolseley Road, Hornsey. The stepped classroom was a feature of the first elementary schools, particularly in cities, to enable children in a very crowded classroom – up to fifty – to see and be seen.

Boys of Wood Green Higher Grade School, 1901. The local authority school provided facilities for fee-paying parents who wanted more than the elementary education for their children. It later became Wood Green County School in Bounds Green Road.

A class in Holy Trinity Infants' School, Tottenham, 1888. The young women standing at the back were pupil teachers learning their profession.

A class in Coleraine Infants' School, Tottenham, 1935. These children are more informally dressed than in the earlier pictures. Most of the girls boast the 'pudding basin' haircuts of the time, rather than long hair. Coleraine was the first Tottenham Board School; built in 1881, it is substantially the same school today.

This picture by a member of Tottenham Camera Club shows a science room in Parkhurst Boys' School, Tottenham, in 1939. Parkhurst was an all-age elementary school, and had started providing specialist teaching for older pupils prior to the introduction of secondary education in 1944.

A carpentry class in Blanche Nevile School, c. 1930. Woodwork had always been part of boys' education, and was further developed as a vocational element of the curriculum to give boys skills in preparation for a manual trade.

The teacher and children are intently watching the speaker's lips in this speech and language class in Blanche Nevile School, *c.* 1946. This specialist school for deaf children was one of the few of its kind in the country. It opened as a class in Bruce Grove School in 1895, moving in 1902 to a large house, The Cedars, in the High Road, and eventually to purpose-built accommodation in Philip Lane, next to the bus garage. It transferred in the 1980s to departments in local mainstream primary and secondary schools.

An art lesson at the Vale School for children with physical disabilities, *c.* 1950. Starting as a class in Parkhurst School in the 1920s, the school transferred in 1928 to purpose-built premises in Vale Road. It has now relocated to bases in local primary and secondary schools.

A young conductor leads the percussionists at the Vale School. Before the war, more than half of the children attending this school suffered from tubercular limbs and heart disease, and fewer than one-third from congenital physical disability.

Tottenham Schools Orchestra rehearsing in Felvus Hall, Tottenham High School for Girls, 1949. Local schools offered all children the percussion instruments seen in Vale Road. Some children also learned other instruments through the peripatetic music service and were brought together to perform as a local orchestra.

Schoolgirls queuing outside the Tottenham mobile school library in 1950. The mobile library service visited all the schools in the district, making available a greater variety of books for young people to borrow and read. Few schools then had an extensive library.

Priory Park in Hornsey, c. 1905. Eight acres of land between Priory Road and Middle Lane were saved from housing development by Hornsey Urban District Council. They were set out as Pleasure Gardens in 1894. Now called Priory Park, it has variously been called Hornsey Gardens, Priory Gardens, Hornsey Pleasure Grounds and Hornsey Recreation Grounds, reflecting the very varied uses to which it was put. Parks such as this one were safe places in which children could play, even without supervision.

The lake at Finsbury Park, *c.* 1905. The park was once part of the extensive Hornsey Wood and was opened as a public park in 1869 by the Metropolitan Board of Works. Although mainly in Hornsey, it was generally regarded as the rural boundary by the people of Islington and Finsbury.

This postcard view of Priory Park in 1908 shows the shrubs and flower beds of the ornamental gardens. This is a sedate scene, with young mothers and their babies. A splendid perambulator is in the foreground.

Lady Henry Somerset, President of the British Women's Temperance Association, opening the drinking fountain in Bruce Castle Park, 1893. The fountain was intended to encourage working people to drink water rather than alcohol, although the main beneficiaries were thirsty children playing in the park.

The fountain was paid for by donations from the Tottenham branch of the BWTA, but has been removed. The coffee stall also opened by the Association is no longer part of the park.

Demonstration of a model railway in Downhills Park in 1952. The park was once the grounds of Downhills House, off Philip Lane. The land was acquired by Tottenham Urban District Council at the end of the nineteenth century following a campaign from local residents.

The model traffic area in Lordship Recreation Ground was opened in 1947 by Tottenham Council to encourage awareness of road safety. Small-scale road systems, junctions and traffic lights made it as realistic as possible. Cars and bikes were hired from the bike shed.

A Tottenham Hebrew Congregation class outing to Epping Forest in 1922. Outings were an exciting feature of school, church and synagogue life for children before the war, usually travelling on horse-drawn brakes.

Children revelling in the floods in Harringay Road, 1937. Not all their childhood was organised into outings and parks! Mostly they played in the streets until the domination of the motor car. The flooded streets were the result of the overflowing streams running from Muswell Hill to the Lea.

Park Lane Nursery in Tottenham, pictured when it was opened in 1940. This was part of a complex that also included child health and dental clinics. Although this picture shows a modern, light design, the buildings have unfortunately not survived; they were demolished in 1997.

Children playing in Park Lane nursery, 1945. The nursery was particularly important during the war, when more women went out to work, as well as during the immediate post-war period of reconstruction.

Children having dinner in Pembury nursery school, *c.* 1945. Pembury nursery was also opened during the war. It took youngsters of three and four, rather than the babies and toddlers who went to the day nurseries.

CHAPTER SIX

RESIDENTS & VISITORS

*Rose Scott, posing for a formal photograph in 1907,
was a member of an ordinary Wood Green and
Tottenham family who had moved into the area from
the crowded streets of Islington. Haringey has long
been an area of immigration from city, country and
overseas. Some of the new residents have stopped for a
few years, others for several generations. A handful are
shown on the following pages, together with a few
visitors. Some of them are well known, but others
represent the ordinary people and families who have
contributed to our community.*

A billboard man parading in Tottenham High Road, *c.* 1900. He is advertising a sports event at the Tee-To Tum grounds, which were established in the grounds of the Gothic House, St Ann's Road, by Edward Rose, a wholesale milliner. The admission price is 1*s* 6*d*, with an 'Al Fresco' concert in the evening. The billboard was a common form of advertising at the time.

Walter Daniel Tull was a successful Spurs footballer between 1908 and 1910, playing inside left. He had been orphaned at the age of nine. During the First World War he became a commissioned officer but was killed in action in 1918.

Stephen Crittin, schoolmaster, pictured with Culvert Road School swimming club in the 1925/6 season. Crittin (back row, left) taught in Tottenham at the time. Better known as Neil Bell the novelist, he also wrote under the name Stephen Southwold.

John Bonny was born in 1875 and was a popular local artist of the naturalist school. He painted many attractive scenes of the still rural parts of Tottenham at the turn of the century.

The poet A.E. Housman was a resident in North Road, Highgate, between 1887 and 1905. His best known poem, 'The Shropshire Lad', was written here.

Charles Bradlaugh, who lived for a time in
Northumberland Park, was elected MP for
Northampton in 1880. He was a well-known free
thinker and is particularly remembered for
refusing to swear the oath when being admitted
to Parliament.

Mrs Mitchell was one of the founders of the Tottenham National Unemployed Workers Movement. She is
seen here walking along Tottenham High Road in 1930 with a Welsh miner. Mrs Mitchell helped to
organise the Tottenham contribution to the hunger marches.

Dr Edward Curtis May pictured in 1870 wearing his distinctive old-fashioned dress. Dr May was a local Quaker who practised in Tottenham between 1822 and 1867. He lived in the house on the High Road now occupied by the British Legion.

Henry Fowler, rates collector, 1880. Together with his father and brother, Fowler collected the rates for the Tottenham Local Board of Health. This early form of local government, together with the money it demanded, was never popular locally.

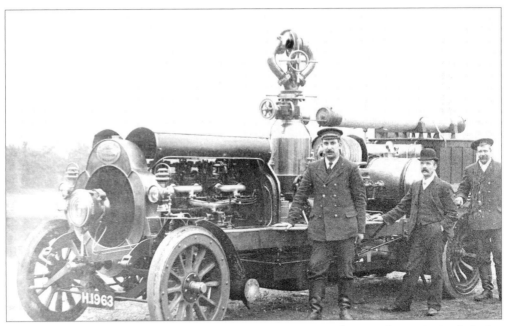

The engineer Mr Zwicky (wearing the bowler hat), pictured on Tottenham Marshes in 1906 with the fire engine he designed for Tottenham Council. Tottenham fire brigade was converted from a volunteer force to a paid one in 1892.

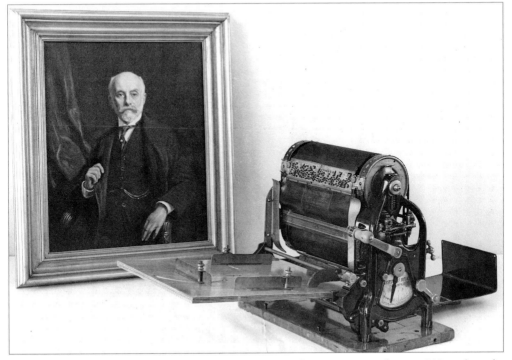

Portrait of David Gestetner, alongside an early duplicator. This picture was taken in 1903 to show the Rotary Cyclostyle duplicator. Gestetner, a Hungarian Jew born in 1854, opened his factory in Broad Lane, Tottenham Hale, in 1904.

The Hunnings brothers, posing with their photography equipment, c. 1860. They took a number of local photographs, including the cricketers on p. 58. Their father, William Hunnings, founded the Tottenham printing works at 516 High Road in 1825. The works later moved to 564 High Road, but it remained a local family firm until eventually moving to Finsbury Park in the 1960s.

Hornsey Council staff, 1914. They were the backbone of local authority administration. They are seen here in the grounds of the council offices, then in Southwood Lane, Highgate. Hornsey became a municipal borough in 1904, and its responsibilities included elementary education, refuse collection, road maintenance, street lighting, drainage and sewage disposal. They also developed amenities such as parks and libraries and started to build council housing in 1892 when still an urban district council. The council offices moved to the Town Hall in Crouch End Broadway in 1935.

Miss Dundee, Lady Superintendent of the
Tottenham Deaconess Institute, 1890. A charity
hospital founded by Dr Laseron in 1868, the
Institute provided training for nurses and care
for the sick. It later became the Prince of Wales
Hospital.

Miss E. Theodora Bickerton, Matron of the
Tottenham Hospital, 1918. Following the death
of Dr Laseron in 1894, the Tottenham Hospital
faced financial difficulties. It was reformed as a
general hospital, managed by a committee
appointed by subscribers.

A 'distinguished visitor' to the Prince of Wales hospital, *c.* 1920. She is believed to be the Princess Louise, Duchess of Argyll, who was then President of the Hospital.

Edward, Prince of Wales, visiting Wood Green underground station in 1933. Pictured here with Lord Ashfield, the prince visited the newly opened station on the Piccadilly line extension. He is walking past the Wood Green offices of Crusha's the printers.

Queen Elizabeth, the Queen Consort, visiting Tottenham salvage works in July 1940. The piggery was started by local refuse workers utilising household waste. It was regarded as an excellent demonstration of conserving food during the war.

Queen Mary inspects the pig waste in August 1940. The waste was called 'Tottenham pudding' and had a particularly rank odour – especially on a hot day in August!

Mr and Mrs Wells and family in front of their home in Kings Terrace, Nightingale Lane, Hornsey, *c.* 1890. They are seen here with Mr Hutt, on the left. Kings Terrace lay between Brook Road and Eastfield Road, and Nightingale Lane then was largely surrounded by open fields.

The Wagerman family of Stainsby Road, Tottenham, 1919/20. The Wagermans were members of the Tottenham Jewish community of the time. Mrs Wagerman owned and ran Philips Stores on the corner of Stainsby and Colsterworth Roads.

CHAPTER SEVEN

THE BOROUGHS IN WARTIME

Charles Greenlees, killed in action in the First World War at the age of twenty-one. War has a tremendous impact on local communities. The Second World War in particular had a devastating effect on the home population. Evacuation, Civil Defence, bombing and the war economy affected every aspect of society, touching young and old, male and female. It was a significant watershed in Haringey's history. Young men went off to war in droves, and many of them would never return. Others were heavily occupied with war work at home.

The 33rd Middlesex Rifle Volunteers on parade on Tottenham Marshes in 1864. A volunteer rifle corps was established by Tottenham residents in 1860, and rifle butts were set up on the marshes for practice.

The walking wounded, some helped by their comrades, are brought to the Prince of Wales hospital in 1914. They were perhaps among the more fortunate, although if their wounds were not too serious then they would soon be back in the trenches.

Evacuee children from Tottenham's Woodlands Park School pictured in Cambridgeshire in 1940. At the outbreak of the Second World War, children throughout London and the suburbs were evacuated to the safety of the countryside.

Evacuees from the same school at a picnic, August 1940. The children do not look very comfortable in this publicity picture from the Ministry of War, perhaps because of the unusually large number of adults present.

Boy with a bomb, 1940. Many homesick children returned from evacuation during the first year to be reunited with their families when the much-feared bombing of civilian targets did not materialise. However, by September 1940 the Blitz had started in earnest. This bomb fell on the Gaumont, Wood Green, in November 1940, but failed to explode.

A Spitfire designated 'Borough of Wood Green'. Local people helped in the production of aircraft through collections and contributions and were rewarded with 'ownership' of a plane such as this.

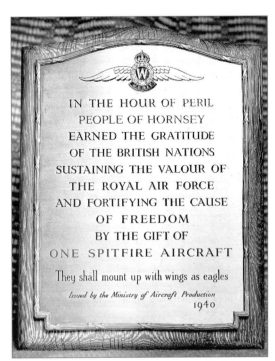

IN THE HOUR OF PERIL
PEOPLE OF HORNSEY
EARNED THE GRATITUDE
OF THE BRITISH NATIONS
SUSTAINING THE VALOUR OF
THE ROYAL AIR FORCE
AND FORTIFYING THE CAUSE
OF FREEDOM
BY THE GIFT OF
ONE SPITFIRE AIRCRAFT

They shall mount up with wings as eagles

Issued by the Ministry of Aircraft Production
1940

The people of Hornsey collected money towards a Spitfire, with a 'thermometer' on Crouch End clock tower to measure the contributions. This plaque was issued in recognition of their efforts.

Anderson shelters being distributed in South Tottenham, April 1939. Made of corrugated iron, the shelters were half-buried in back gardens for use by individual families, and were able to survive anything but a direct hit.

The warden's post, Bruce Grove almshouses, 1945. To the right is a trench shelter, a larger shelter than the Anderson, for all the residents of the almshouses.

Bombed houses in West Beech and Bury Road, 1944. The houses in the foreground have been completely demolished, with even the shelters barely remaining. People in the shelters were either killed or severely injured, but there was one emotional rescue. A family was found alive in the rubble and air was pumped in as the rescuers fought to free them. A young boy in the shelter talked to the rescuers throughout the operation, reporting 'all well' at frequent intervals until about five minutes before he was reached. Then he said 'mummy has fallen asleep'. His mother was a fatality, but he and his father survived.

A rescue operation in Tottenham Lane, 1944. Civil Defence workers and their dog try to locate survivors following the devastating effect of a V2 rocket explosion. Ten people were killed and seventy-eight injured in this incident.

The effect of a V2 rocket attack, Sydney Road, Hornsey, January 1945. Only the party walls were left standing, while the houses opposite were completely demolished. The V2 rockets launched on London from June 1944 were particularly feared as they gave little warning of their approach.

Hornsey Civil Defence team assembled outside Crouch End Town Hall in September 1939 to hear Prime Minister Neville Chamberlain's declaration of war. Until 1943 Civil Defence was voluntary, and a quarter of its members were women. These volunteers were a key part of the defence strategy, operating mobile medical units, carrying out fire-watching duties or patrolling the streets as wardens, often at considerable personal risk. Many also had day jobs, but worked duty shifts at night.

A Civil Defence ambulance driver poses with her ambulance. Women played a large part in the war effort on the home front, both in defence and also in production. At first their employment in factories, Civil Defence and the forces was voluntary, but conscription of unmarried women between the ages of twenty and thirty was introduced in 1941 for 'vital war work'.

The Civil Defence report and control desk, located in the basement of the Tottenham Polytechnic, pictured in 1945. On the left is Mr Field, the resources clerk, with Mr H.E. Rosen, OC Control, on the right.

This Civil Defence complex in Tottenham High Road was built on the site of the old Reynardsons Almshouses, opposite the Palace Theatre. On the left is a typical static water reservoir, used for firefighting.

Wartime salvage collection in Tottenham. With a severe shortage of raw and manufactured goods, and a large proportion of industrial production devoted to armaments, salvage and recycling of all sorts was crucial during the war.

Aluminium collection for the war effort at the Central Library in 1940. The women in this picture are members of the Tottenham branch of the Women's Voluntary Service, founded in 1938.

A wartime Christmas party, complete with party hats and Christmas crackers, held in the basement of Bruce Castle Museum in 1940. It was typical of people's determination to carry on as normal. On the right is Mr Warren, the museum technician, who hosted the party.

This mural decoration in the dining-room at Devonshire Hill School tells the story of Cinderella. It was painted in 1944 by Vanessa Bell and Duncan Grant and sponsored by the Council for the Encouragement of Music and the Arts.

Prefab housing in White Hart Lane in 1950. Soldiers returning home from the First World War had faced a desperate housing shortage, but this was even more of a problem after the Second World War, owing to the devastating effect of bombing. Prefabs – constructed in the factory and erected on site – were one answer. They were supposed to be temporary but they were popular and comfortable, and endured for a long while after the war.

CHAPTER EIGHT

EVENTS & CELEBRATIONS

The opportunity to celebrate as a community was always a welcome break from everyday life and often provided a much-needed boost to morale. National events, such as peace celebrations and coronations, were commemorated locally with street parties and parades. This is Lorenco Road in Tottenham, a particularly poor street, which won an award for the best decorated street during the coronation festivities of 1953. Other occasions were celebrations of local events, confirming pride in the achievements of the civic community or a celebration of mutual help with fund-raising carnivals.

Beating the bounds at Alexandra Palace in 1893. Wood Green and Alexandra Palace still marked the western border of Tottenham at this date, before Wood Green became a separate urban district council in 1894.

Boys prepare to swim the Lea, marking the eastern boundary of Tottenham parish, to beat the bounds. Walking the bounds of a parish to ensure landowners remained within their property and kept fences in good order was an ancient custom; it had largely died out by the end of the nineteenth century.

Peace Day in July 1919 was a day of national celebrations, and the Peace Pageant performed by the school children of Wood Green was particularly spectacular. The pageant celebrated key moments in Wood Green's history, including a visit from Queen Elizabeth I in 1590, the opening of the New River in 1618, and independence from Tottenham in 1894. Here we see Boudicca on her way from St Albans to London, via Wood Green, during her rebellion against the Romans. The children were from Muswell Hill School in Frobisher Road, directed by their teacher Miss Mountain.

On the day before the pageant, there was a procession, with children dressed up in historical costume. The costumes were made by teachers and parents to ensure the minimum of expense. These children – a coster family with cart – are outside Wood Green County School (see p. 76).

Young children – probably the Lynwood Orchestra under Miss Beecroft – performing for the Wood Green Peace Pageant in 1919.

The peace celebrations in Tottenham in 1919 were marked by local street parties, such as this one in Steele Road. The local children have put on a good display with their fancy dress costumes.

The 1945 peace was celebrated in Haringey with street parties, such as this one in Glenwood Road. Collections, including ration tickets, were organised in the local neighbourhoods and food laid out on the trestle tables in the street.

Young people from the Coldfall estate, Hornsey, preparing for the coronation celebrations for George VI in May 1937. Hornsey celebrated the coronation with a parade of decorated floats through the streets. Starting in Muswell Hill, where this picture was taken just off Grand Avenue, the parade finished with a fair in Priory Park. The Coldfall children received first prize for children's emblematic floats. Theirs was called a study in red, white and blue.

(Opposite top) Winchelsea Road, Tottenham, becomes a traffic-free zone for a street party celebration – this time for the coronation of Queen Elizabeth in 1953. This party seems to have attracted as many onlookers as participants, and there are significantly more men to be seen than in the earlier post-war picture on p. 121.

(Opposite bottom) Janson's Road in Tottenham provided entertainment for the children during the 1953 coronation. Although the picture looks sunny, the day was recorded by the *Tottenham Herald* as being 'rain soaked and windswept'.

Procession of Yeomanry at the opening of Bruce Castle Park, 1892. They are coming down Tottenham High Road towards Bruce Grove. Bruce Castle and its grounds were acquired by Tottenham UDC in 1891 (see p. 16).

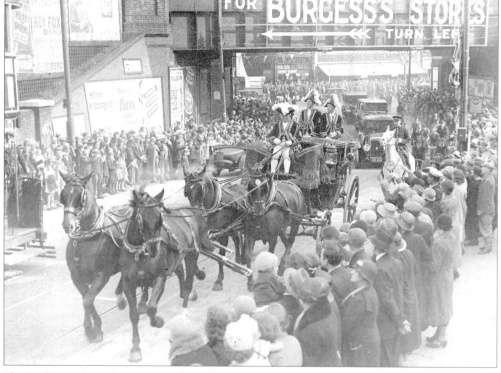

The Lord Mayor's coach moves smartly to the Children's Display at Downhills Park in the Charter Day procession. Tottenham received its charter to become a Municipal Borough in 1934.

Tottenham Hospital carnival committee, 1882. This rather serious group of local worthies helped to organise the annual carnival to raise money for the local hospital (see pp. 126 and 134). Back row, left to right: Mr Drewett, Mr Nash, Mr Bradbury, Mr Cook, Mr Hurst; front row: Mr Malone, Mr Jubb, Mr Crane, Mr Combes.

Miss Pearl Webb was Tottenham Carnival Queen in 1939. She is seen here receiving purses for local charities at Billy Smart's Fair in Bruce Castle Park.

Young children in fancy dress are waiting to join the 1901 Carnival procession organised by the austere gentlemen pictured on the previous page. This picture was taken by Fred Fisk outside no. 537 in Tottenham High Road. It is still early in the day, and the shops are shuttered. As well as a public occasion, the carnival raised money to contribute to the amenities in the local hospital, such as the Carnival Bed (see p. 134).

The formal opening in 1908 of Wood Green refuse destructor (see p. 26). In the background on the left is Alexandra School, with Barratt's sweet factory on the right.

The Hibbert sisters replaced three trees at Seven Sisters in 1928. As early as 1631 the Tottenham historian Bedwell recorded the magnificent walnut tree, encircled by elms, standing on Page Green Common, Broad Lane. The trees have been replaced several times since then. Called the 'seven sisters', they gave their name to the road built in 1833.

The opening of the Home and Colonial Training College, Wood Green, 1904. This splendid building in Lordship Lane (see p. 158) was previously the Royal Masonic School.

The funeral of a fireman on Tottenham High Road in 1924. He was killed when his fire engine collided with a tram car. The parade is passing near Spurs ground, with the buildings of Klinger's hosiery factory on the right.

The opening of the Stuart Villas centre in Stuart Crescent, 1918. Shown here are members of the Wood Green Council Education Committee and the Day Nursery Committee, together with some of the nursery children. Stuart Crescent had a day nursery for children under school age whose mothers were 'compelled to go out to work' (probably war widows). There was also an ante-natal clinic, dental clinic and ophthalmic clinic, and it continues today on the same site as Stuart Crescent Health Centre.

Danny Blanchflower,
captain of Spurs,
celebrates his team's
FA Cup victory in 1962.
Mrs Herbert, wife of the
mayor Alderman
W.J. Herbert, is holding
the cup.

Crowds gather outside the Tottenham Royal (formerly the Canadian Rink, see p. 63) to celebrate Spurs' victory in 1962. This picture marks the heyday of the Royal Dance Hall – and perhaps of Spurs as well!

CHAPTER NINE

CARING FOR THE COMMUNITY

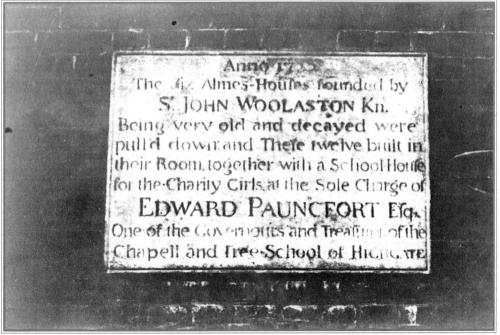

Almshouses were erected to provide decent homes for those too old or infirm to provide for themselves. They were often funded by local benefactors, and this plaque commemorates the gifts from two individuals who helped to build the almshouses in Southwood Lane, Highgate, shown on p. 141. State provision has now largely replaced the voluntary and charitable work that financed hospitals and supported care for the elderly illustrated on the following pages.

The Deaconess Institute, later the Prince of Wales Hospital, Tottenham Green, photographed by Fisk in 1886. The hospital was founded by Dr Laseron in 1868 (see p. 98). In the foreground is a coal cart.

Passmore Edwards Hospital, Wood Green, was established in 1895, with twenty-five beds for non-infectious cases. Infectious patients, such as those with smallpox and scarlet fever, went to fever hospitals at St Ann's, Tottenham, and Coppett's Wood, Hornsey. Passmore Edwards was also maintained by voluntary contributions.

Hornsey Cottage Hospital, Park Road, 1911. This hospital was opened for non-infectious patients of the 'lower middle class of Hornsey' following a difficult period of fund-raising. The hospital has managed to survive reorganisation, unlike its counterparts in Wood Green and Hornsey.

A group of nursing staff from Hornsey Hospital pose for a picture in 1911. A nurses' home was added in 1930 to provide accommodation.

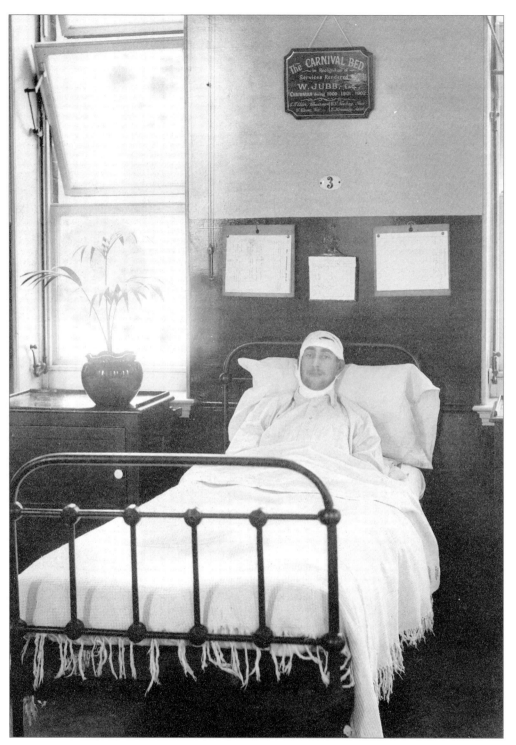

A patient enjoying the benefits of the Carnival Bed in the Prince of Wales Hospital. The bed was one of those established from the proceeds of the Carnival. It commemorates a former chairman of the committee, W. Jubb, pictured on p. 125.

The Jewish Home and Hospital for Incurables, Tottenham High Road. Built in 1901, this voluntary hospital was established by fund-raising in the Jewish community to provide care for the long-term sick and disabled of all ages. It was built within easy reach of the East End in what was then pleasantly open surroundings.

The elegant and spacious Jewish Hospital had an equally elegant interior. This picture, taken shortly after it opened, shows a women's group enjoying a musical session.

Public Health Department staff enjoying an outing, 1904. Local Health Boards played a key role in ensuring that the rapid development of houses, streets and factories was contained within limits to ensure health and safety. The Board was particularly successful in keeping the streets wide and spacious in Hornsey.

A ratcatcher setting his traps alongside the Moselle Brook in Downhills Park, 1928. This was another, less enviable, aspect of public health. Rough clothes were needed for this work.

A woman ironing in a Tottenham municipal laundry. Two laundries were opened in Bromley Road and Tiverton Road in 1932 to provide good quality washing facilities in the days before launderettes and washing machines.

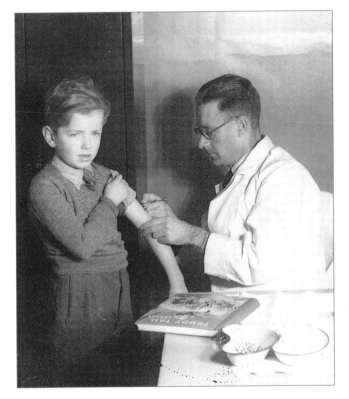

A child being immunised in 1948. The local boroughs such as Hornsey had started immunisation in 1936, but it was not until the national campaign in 1941 that fatal diseases such as diphtheria started to be eliminated.

In 1952 the Tottenham Old People's Welfare Committee organised an old age pensioners' outing to the BBC. The committee was very active during the post-war decades, raising funds from local firms and groups, including Spurs, as well as from individuals. They provided concerts, Christmas parties, outings, holidays – and even a chiropodist. They also organised the clubs and subsidised meals shown on the opposite page.

(Opposite top) A meal delivery provided by the Old People's Welfare Committee in the 1950s. The meals were prepared by Tottenham Council at a subsidised cost to the committee, which distributed them to pensioners. In 1958 the charge was 1s a meal. The old age pension in 1956 was £2 a week.

(Opposite bottom) A 'whist drive' in session with a dedicated group of players. This pensioners' club in High Cross church hall is shown in the early 1950s.

Sanchez Almshouses, 1907. The Quaker Meeting House is in the background. These almshouses were built by Balthazar Sanchez, a Spanish confectioner who lived in Tottenham in the late sixteenth century. They were declared unfit for habitation in 1905, by which time the land they stood on had sunk below the level of the road.

Hornsey almshouses in 1890 boasted thatched roofs and long front gardens. These parish cottages, demolished by 1898, were on the Bowling Alley estate in Hornsey village.

Drapers Almshouses, Bruce Grove, 1908. They look substantially as they do today after renovation. They were built by the Sailmakers (later the Drapers) Company in 1868 at the top of Bruce Grove, where it narrowed to a rambling country lane.

Sir John Wollaston Almshouses, Southwood Lane, Highgate, 1908. The original houses, built in the seventeenth century, were rebuilt in 1722 with the help of a bequest from Edward Pauncefort. They provided twelve homes and a girls' charity school.

Printers Almshouses, Wood Green, 1913. They were built on the High Road at the junction of Bounds Green in 1849 for members of the printing trade, with homes for twelve people in what was then a pleasant rural environment.

The Fishmongers Almshouses, Wood Green, were also built in 1849 by the Fishmongers and Poulterers Societies in 'a locality unsurpassed for salubrity of air by any within the like distance of the metropolis'. The site is now occupied by Haringey Civic Centre.

CHAPTER TEN

LANDMARKS
PAST & PRESENT

*The Crouch End clock tower was ceremoniously opened in
1895 to commemorate Mr H.R. Williams, a leading
local Liberal politician. One of his successful campaigns
was to save Highgate Woods. The clock tower, opposite
Topsfield Parade, is still a focal point of the district, as
are some of the other landmarks shown on the following
pages. However, many of the churches, grand houses and
civic buildings have been demolished or become lost
within the network of roads and buildings now
surrounding them.*

Tottenham High Cross, 1890s. This area has been known as Tottenham High Cross since the Middle Ages. This cross, built in 1809, replaced an earlier wooden one, and is now an isolated monument in the centre of a busy modern road system.

St James's Church, Muswell Hill, dominates this 1950s scene of Edwardian shops on the Broadway. There has been a church on this site since 1842. This church was built in 1902 to accommodate the growing population of the area.

This snowy photograph shows the view along Tottenham Lane towards Hornsey parish church in 1889. The tower of St Mary's Church dates from about 1500. The nave was built in 1832, but fell into disuse in 1889 when a new church was built alongside. The nave was demolished in 1927 and the new church in 1969, leaving the medieval tower standing in isolation.

All Hallows Church, Tottenham, 1900. There has been a church on this site from the twelfth century, and it was dedicated to All Hallows in the fifteenth century. There have been many alterations, including a restoration by William Butterfield in 1875. William Bedwell, translator of the King James Bible, was vicar there from 1607 to 1632.

The Quaker Meeting House in Tottenham High Road, 1909. Built in 1715 for what was then a substantial and wealthy community of Quakers, the meeting house was rebuilt in 1809 but demolished for redevelopment in the 1960s.

'Deseret' Church of the Latter-Day Saints, 1908. Standing on the corner of Crowland Road and the High Road in South Tottenham, it was built in 1893. It was intended to be a public house but the owners were never able to obtain a licence. It was opened as the missionary headquarters of the Mormon Church in 1908 amid considerable controversy. It remained the church's headquarters until 1927.

Alexandra Palace was opened in 1873 and demolished by fire just ten days later. This first building, intended to emulate south London's Crystal Palace, was built in a park converted from farmland in 1863.

The second Alexandra Palace showing the BBC television mast erected in 1935. The palace was built on high ground in the park, with magnificent views across London. Television broadcasting started from there in 1936.

Alexandra Palace after the devastating fire in 1873. It was soon rebuilt, however, and opened again in 1875. This started a period of growth and development for the Palace and the park, as well as for Wood Green. The Great Hall in the centre, with its grand organ, could seat up to 12,000 people for concerts. It was flanked by courts on the east and west sides and glass-roofed conservatories. A particular attraction was the monkey house and zoo, housed in the Palm Court.

Alexandra Palace ablaze again in 1980. The Palace has been dogged by misfortune, and its survival has often been a matter of doubt. The popular lake in the park was earmarked for housing development in 1900 but it was saved by a consortium of local authorities, which redeveloped the Palace and park in 1901. The park covers nearly 200 acres. The many leisure facilities have included roller-skating, bowls and concerts inside the Palace, and funfairs and circuses in the park, with even at one time a racecourse.

(Opposite top) Bruce Castle, shown here around 1870, was built early in the sixteenth century as the manor house for Tottenham. In the nineteenth century it was used as a private boarding school for middle-class boys. It was run by the family of Rowland Hill, the originator of the penny post.

(Opposite bottom) Bruce Castle looks particularly dramatic when floodlit at night, giving it particular prominence in its position near the junction of Lordship Lane and Bruce Grove. The building has been owned by the local authority since 1891.

Archway Bridge, 1885. The bridge was built in 1813 to carry Hornsey Lane over the recently constructed Archway Road, bypassing the steep gradient of Highgate Hill. Developers originally tried to tunnel through the hill, but the collapse of the tunnel led to the alternative solution of a cutting.

The Priory in Hornsey, *c.* 1890. It was built in the Gothic style by Jacob Warner and owned by the Warner family throughout the nineteenth century. Its site was later occupied by Redston, Danvers and Warner Roads, Park Avenue North and Priory Avenue.

Muswell Lodge, Tetherdown, *c.* 1900. This house was the scene of a dramatic murder in 1896. The owner, Henry Smith, who lived alone, was killed by burglars who were later arrested after a 'desperate resistance'.

The Lodge in Woodside Park, Wood Green, was built in 1822. It was originally the gatehouse for Chitts House (now the site of Sylvan Road). It was last occupied in 1890, but it remains, now in council ownership, one of the oldest buildings in Wood Green.

The Elms, Wood Green, stood behind Gladstone Gardens in the High Road, opposite Gladstone Avenue. Both the gardens and house were redeveloped in the 1930s forming the site of the shops of Broadway Parade and Odeon cinema.

The Mansion, Alexandra Park Road. This grandly named house backed on to Alexandra Park, opposite
Palace Gates Road, and was built between 1870 and 1890. Alexandra Park Road, running from Colney
Hatch Lane to Wood Green station, was laid out by the 1890s, but the Mansion stood in splendid isolation
for many more years, until succumbing to the gradual encroachment of more modest suburban houses.

Rectory House in White Hart Lane, pictured after a heavy fall of snow. Also known as the Moat House, it stood in Tottenham Park on the south side of White Hart Lane. The house was demolished in 1904 and the land was intended for building development. However, it was opened instead for sports, including cricket and tennis, and then later as allotments. The land now forms part of the extensive Tottenham cemetery.

(Opposite top) The gas showrooms in Tottenham High Road, shown here in 1910, are now local council offices. They were opened in 1901 to demonstrate the benefits of the new gas lamps, cookers and fires.

(Opposite bottom) The London Co-operative Society department store stands opposite the gas showrooms on the corner of Lansdowne Road. It was built in 1930, when this picture was taken, and was one of three department stores then in Tottenham. The others were Burgess's, built on the site of the Sanchez almshouses (see p. 140), and Ward's, on the corner of Seven Sisters and the High Road.

Wood Green Public Library, on the corner of Station Road and the High Road, 1910. It was built with money donated by Andrew Carnegie, the American philanthropist, but was demolished in 1973 to make way for an office block.

Woodall House, headquarters of the gas company, 1930. This impressive building on Lordship Lane was previously the Home and Colonial Training College and before that the Royal Masonic School (see p. 128). It is now a Crown Court.

INDEX